100 QUESTIONS AND ANSWERS

FOOTBALL

Written by
Neil Cook and Paul Harrison

Designed by
**Deborah Chadwick and
Chris Dymond**

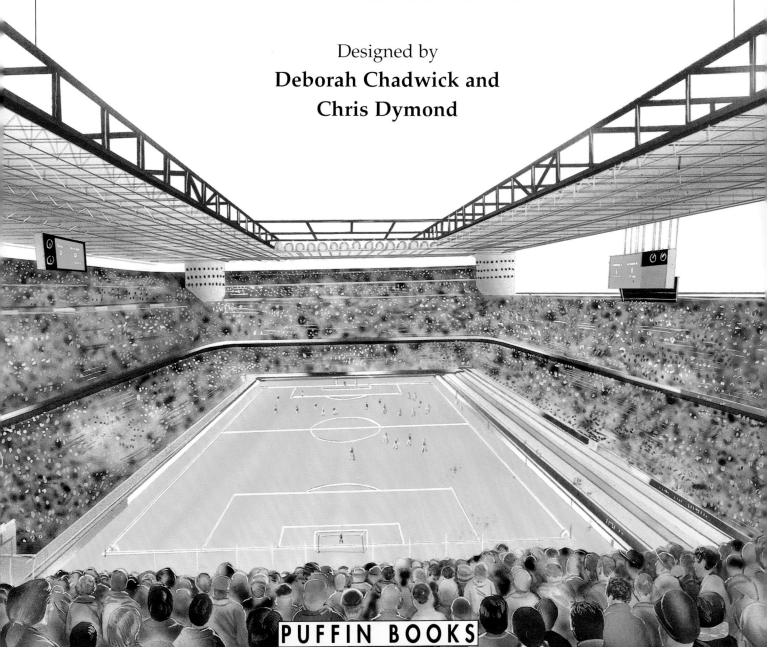

PUFFIN BOOKS

Neil Cook studied English and American literature at Manchester University. He has published articles on a number of sports and is currently involved in computer sports simulation projects.

PUFFIN BOOKS

Published by the Penguin Group
Penguin Books Ltd, 27 Wrights Lane, London W8 5TZ, England
Penguin Books USA Inc., 375 Hudson Street, New York, New York 10014, USA
Penguin Books Australia Ltd, Ringwood, Victoria, Australia
Penguin Books Canada Ltd, 10 Alcorn Avenue, Toronto, Ontario, Canada M4V 3B2
Penguin Books (NZ) Ltd, 182-190 Wairau Road, Auckland 10, New Zealand

Penguin Books Ltd, Registered Offices: Harmondsworth, Middlesex, England

First published 1995
10 9 8 7 6 5 4

Produced for Puffin Books by Zigzag Publishing, a division of Quadrillion Publishing Ltd., Godalming Business Centre, Woolsack Way, Godalming, Surrey GU7 1XW

Series concept: Tony Potter
Editor: Paul Harrison
Managing Editor: Nicola Wright
Production: Zoë Fawcett and Simon Eaton
Illustrated by: Peter Dennis, Peter Bull, Jeremy Gower, Ed Org, Hemesh Alles
Cover design: Deborah Chadwick
Cover illustration: Tim Gill

Colour separations: Sussex Repro, England
Printed in Singapore

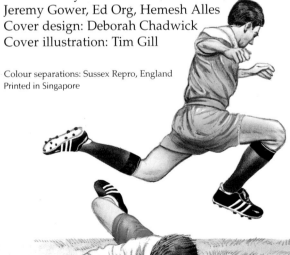

Contents

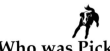

Have you ever wondered who were the first people to play football? Do you know what 'mob football' was? Who are the Socceroos? What was special about William Foulkes?

This book will provide the answers to these and any other questions that you might ask about football. You will find out all about the history of football and discover who the great players are, those in the past as well as the present. You can also encounter the different sorts of league and cup competitions from around the world.

With the aid of colourful diagrams and clear instructions you will be able to practise a range of football skills, such as swerving the ball through the air and scoring goals. You will also find lots of other useful information that will help you to improve your game.

During the 1800s it was common to see men playing football wearing top hats!

How did football begin?

A kind of football was played in Ancient China as early as 200 BC. The Ancient Romans and Greeks also played versions of football. However, these games looked more like modern-day rugby than the game of football played today.

Q When was football first played in Britain?

A It seems likely that the Ancient Romans introduced their version of football, called 'harpastum', to Britain around AD 200.

Q Was football always popular?

A Football has actually been banned on a number of different occasions through history. In 1365 King Edward III banned football because he claimed his soldiers preferred football to fighting. Football has also been banned because shop windows and buildings were often broken or damaged during unruly games of mob football.

Q What was 'mob football'?

A Mob football was the term given to the type of football played in the Middle Ages. Football games were traditionally played on Shrove Tuesday (Pancake Day), with up to 500 people taking part. The 'pitches' were the length of a town or from village to village. The games would last all day and could be very violent. Sometimes people were even killed!

Before 1891 there were no linesmen as we know today, and the referee did not stand on the pitch. Each team provided an umpire who acted as a linesman. The referee's job was to make decisions when the two umpires disagreed.

Q Have football strips changed much?

A Early football strips consisted of long-sleeved jerseys, knickerbockers tucked into long socks and often a hat that resembled a nightcap. Strips progressed from knickerbockers to baggy shorts to the more streamlined outfits used today.

1890s   1930s   1990s

Q When were the first rules written?

A There were a number of different sets of rules before the formation of the Football Association (FA). The Association, a group of leading football clubs, finally agreed a common set of rules on the 8th December 1865. These were the basis of the game played today.

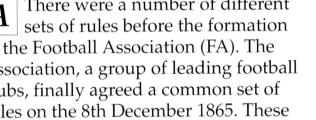

Q When did league football begin?

A William McGregor organised the first football league on 2nd March 1888 when he invited the leading clubs in England to join a league. The twelve clubs that formed the first league were Accrington, Aston Villa, Blackburn Rovers, Bolton Wanderers, Burnley, Derby County, Everton, Notts County, Preston North End, Stoke, West Bromwich Albion and Wolverhampton Wanderers.

Q Who was JA Brodie?

A In 1890 JA Brodie invented and patented goal nets. Until that time goals did not have nets which could result in confusion as to whether a goal had been scored or not. It was only five years earlier that crossbars replaced tape between goalposts.

The Greeks used inflated pigs' bladders to play football.

What rules are there?

Football has many rules to ensure that the game is played fairly and correctly. Players who break the rules are penalised and may even be sent off the pitch.

Pie chart: 120 — Extra Time — First Half — 90 — Second Half — Half Time — 45

Q How long is a game of football?

A A game of football lasts 90 minutes. It is split into two halves of 45 minutes each. In some cases extra time is played to decide a winner. Then a match lasts for 120 minutes.

Q What are all the lines on the pitch for?

A They divide the pitch into different areas, so that the players and referee know where the ball should be placed at different times.

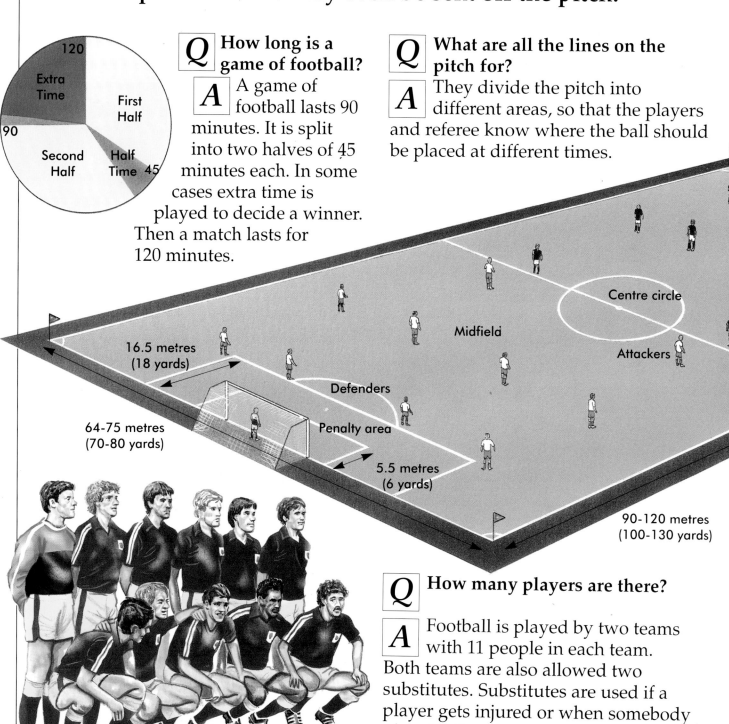

16.5 metres (18 yards)

Centre circle

Midfield

Attackers

Defenders

Penalty area

5.5 metres (6 yards)

64-75 metres (70-80 yards)

90-120 metres (100-130 yards)

Q How many players are there?

A Football is played by two teams with 11 people in each team. Both teams are also allowed two substitutes. Substitutes are used if a player gets injured or when somebody plays badly.

The rules say that the ball must be between 68 and 71 cm in circumference. The circumference is the distance around the outside of the ball.

Guiseppe Lorenzo of Bologna was sent off after only ten seconds in a game against Parma in 1990.

Q What do all the players do?

A It is the goalkeeper's job to protect the goal, and he is the only player allowed to touch the ball with his hands. Defenders are there to stop the other team from getting close enough to score. The midfield players must win the ball by tackling the opposition and passing it to the attackers. It is the job of the attackers to score goals.

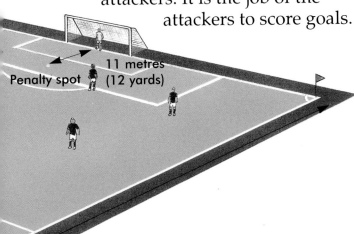

Penalty spot — 11 metres (12 yards)

Q What is 'off-side'?

A There must be at least two defenders between an attacker and the goal when the attacker gets the ball from a team mate. If not, this is 'off-side', and the defending team gets a free kick. Players cannot be off-side in their own half of the pitch from a free kick, a throw-in, or a corner kick.

Q What are red and yellow cards for?

A A referee shows a player a yellow card if the player continues to break the rules. A player is shown the red card for violent play, using foul language or for committing a foul after being shown a yellow card. When a player is shown a red card they have to leave the field.

Q When does the referee give a free kick?

A There are two sorts of free kick, direct and indirect. Direct free kicks are given for fouls, violent play and hand ball. Indirect free kick offences include off-side and time wasting by the goalkeeper. If a player commits an offence worth a direct free kick in his own penalty area, the referee awards a penalty.

Q When do you know if you have scored a goal?

A The whole of the ball must cross the goal line before the referee can blow his whistle to signal a goal.

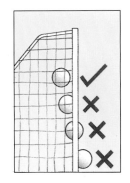

How do you control the ball?

In 1988, Allan Abutu Nyanjong of Kenya kept a football off the ground without using his hands for 16 hours 27 minutes.

There are different ways of controlling the ball when passing, shooting and goalkeeping. A good control of the ball demands a lot of practice and skill.

Q Which is the best foot to kick with?

A Most of the time left-handed people are stronger with their left foot and right-handed people stronger with their right foot. Ideally players should be able to pass the ball with both feet, so they concentrate on strengthening their weaker side.

Q What is the best way to pass accurately?

A For an accurate short pass, use the inside of the strongest foot. Angle the kicking foot away from your body and strike the ball in the middle. For a longer air-borne pass hit the bottom of the ball with the top of the foot and follow through with the kicking foot.

Close-up view

Q What is the best way to score?

A Place the weaker foot alongside the ball and angle the kicking foot down. Lean back with the body and strike the ball in the middle. The kicking foot should follow through in the direction of the goal.

Close-up view

Q How do you control the ball when running?

A When running with the ball, kick it far enough so that you do not have to slow down, but not so far that other players can reach it before you do.

Q Which parts of the body can a player use to hit the ball?

A Players can use any part of their body except their arms or hands.

After the ball has been kicked your foot should continue to move forward in the direction that the ball has gone. This is called the 'follow through' and it adds power to your kick.

Q How do you swerve a ball?

A Swerving the ball in the air is a difficult skill that takes a lot of practice. The kicking foot must be kept straight and the ball hit with the side of the foot. You must kick the side of the ball and have a good follow through.

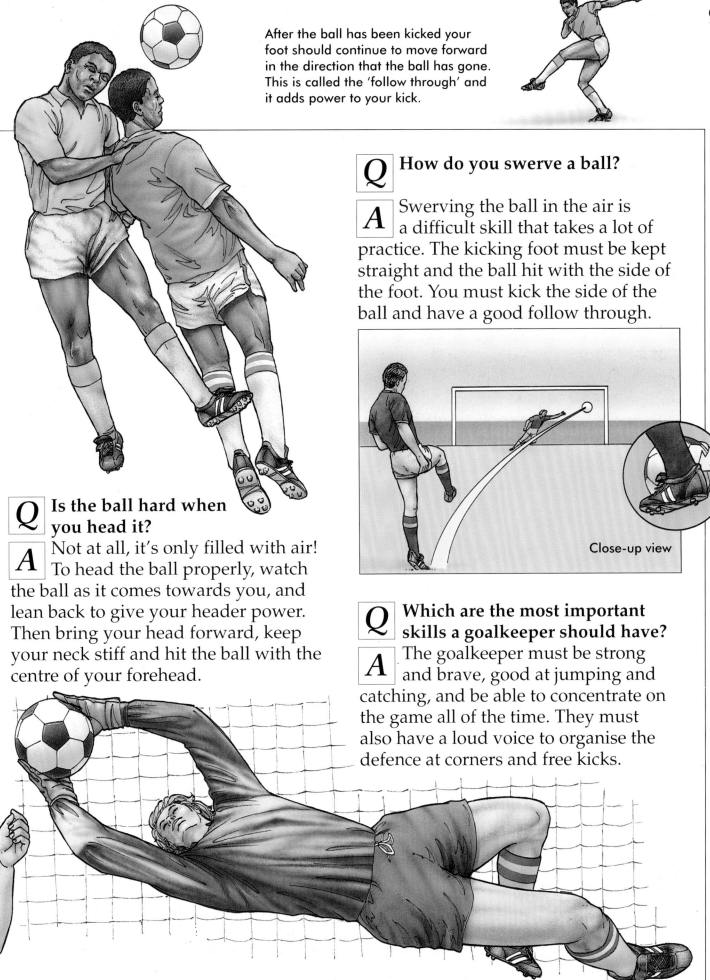

Close-up view

Q Is the ball hard when you head it?

A Not at all, it's only filled with air! To head the ball properly, watch the ball as it comes towards you, and lean back to give your header power. Then bring your head forward, keep your neck stiff and hit the ball with the centre of your forehead.

Q Which are the most important skills a goalkeeper should have?

A The goalkeeper must be strong and brave, good at jumping and catching, and be able to concentrate on the game all of the time. They must also have a loud voice to organise the defence at corners and free kicks.

How should you train?

To be a good footballer you need to develop your skill, strength and stamina. Young players should practise the basic skills needed to pass, shoot and head the ball. Practice is the key to learning any new skill - what first seems difficult soon becomes second nature.

Q How can I strengthen my legs?

A Build up your legs with repeated short sprints of no more than 25 metres. Most of the running in a football match is made up of short sprints such as this. Turn sharply at the end of each sprint and run back the way you came - being able to turn quickly is an important part of the game.

Q What should you eat to stay fit?

A A good diet is very important. Avoid fatty foods, such as crisps and fried food. Fizzy drinks and sweets are also not good for you. You should eat fresh fruit and grilled food. Rather than eating white bread and drinking full fat milk, eat brown bread and semi-skimmed milk instead.

Q How do you improve your stamina?

A You can improve your stamina, or staying power, by doing exercise, such as running and cycling.

Q What helps to improve ball control?

A Pass a ball to a friend without letting it touch the ground, using feet, thighs, chest and head. If there is a tennis court near by, pass the ball the same way over the net. Improve your heading skills by getting a friend to throw a ball in the air for you to head it back in to their hands.

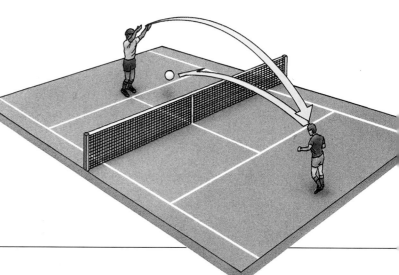

The England squad train at Lilleshall Hall in Shropshire. This is the home of the FA's training centre and the Rehabilitation and Sports Injury Centre. It was paid for by a donation from South Africa as a thank you present for Britain's help in the Second World War.

Q **Can you practise by yourself?**

A Practise keeping the ball in the air using your feet, thighs or head. Keep a chart of how long you kept the ball off the ground and you will see how you improve over a few weeks.

Q **Are there any games to improve football skills?**

A There are many games that you can play to improve your skills. One of the most popular is *60-seconds*, where a player has a minute to beat the goalkeeper with a volley or half-volley. Another popular game is *One-touch*, where players are allowed one touch to pass the ball to other team mates.

Q **Why do players stretch before a game?**

A Players stretch and run around before a game to warm up. Warming up is important as it loosens the muscles and helps to prevent injuries. Warm-up exercises should be supervised by a knowledgeable adult.

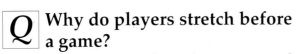

The most successful manager was Bob Paisley who won six division titles and eight cups with Liverpool.

How do teams play?

I t is important that all players know their position, the team's formation and the tactics they are using to win. This is all part of the planning process that goes on before a game.

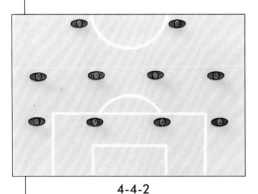

4-4-2

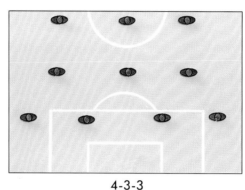

4-3-3

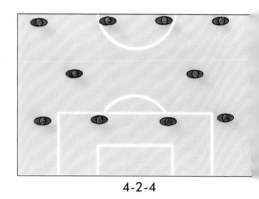

4-2-4

Q What is a team's formation?

A The formation is the way the 10 outfield players are arranged on the pitch. Most teams play with at least four players in defence to avoid giving goals away. However, players need to be spread quite evenly across the pitch. The most common formations include 4-4-2, 4-3-3, and 4-2-4.

Q What are set plays?

A Set plays are specially organised routines used by the attacking team during free kicks and corners. As the opposition must be nine metres (10 yards) from the ball at a free kick it allows a player the time to do something really special or skilful, such as a clever pass or a swerving shot.

'Total football' was a style of play pioneered by the excellent Dutch side of the 1970s. It relied upon very skilful players being able to play in a number of different positions. This meant that opposing teams were never sure which players they should be defending against during Dutch attacks.

Q How do teams play in Britain?

A Football in Britain is played at a very fast pace. The players are quick and have a lot of stamina. Players get tackled in midfield before they threaten the opposition's goal, and then play long passes in the air. Attackers need to be tall, strong, and good at heading. Defenders tend to defend an area of the pitch rather than mark an individual attacker.

Q Do teams play differently elsewhere?

A In Europe attacks are built up more slowly. Short passes are played to the feet of team mates. Each defender usually stays close to one attacker rather than defending a zone. Often they play with a sweeper, an extra defensive player who is also used to start attacks.

Q Who decides the team's tactics?

A This is the job of the manager, who is the most important person at the football club. A manager picks the team, works with the players during training to see who is the best, and develops set plays. If the manager picks the wrong players or uses the wrong tactics, the team is unlikely to win.

Q Does the manager own the club?

A Even football managers have bosses. Most big clubs are owned by a group of rich people and have a Board of Directors and a Chairman. The managers must do their job well or the Chairmen could sack them. The Manager must also convince the Chairman to give money to buy new players.

Q Which is the best way to play?

A The best British teams combine the strength and stamina of the British game with skill and control seen elsewhere. Liverpool in the 1980s and Manchester United in the 1990s are good examples of such teams.

Quick running and accurate passing are the signs of a good team.

The most successful side ever was Penlake Junior FC who went 153 games without defeat!

Which are the best teams?

There have been many great teams in the history of football and it is very difficult to compare teams from different countries. It is easier to compare teams that play in the same country at the same time.

Q Which is the most successful English club?

A Liverpool has won the First Division (now the Premiership) title 18 times. Their greatest success came under the managers Bill Shankly and Bob Paisley from the 1960s to the 1980s. They have also won the European Cup four times.

Q When did an English side first win the European Cup?

A Manchester United won the trophy in 1968. The Red Devils, as the team was known, dominated English football during the 1960s under the management of Sir Matt Busby. The team included great players, such as Bobby Charlton, George Best and Denis Law.

Sir Matt Busby

Sir Bobby Charlton

Q Which was the first British club to win the European Cup?

A Celtic were European Cup winners in 1967. They also won the Scottish First Division Championship and the Scottish Cup the same year.

George Best

Denis Law

On the 6th February 1958 an aeroplane crash in Munich killed most of 'Busby's Babes', Manchester United's exciting side of the 1950s. Survivors of the crash, such as Sir Matt Busby and Sir Bobby Charlton, went on to build the great team of the 1960s.

Q Which is the best European side?

A Many people think that the Spanish club Real Madrid were the best ever in the late 1950s and early 1960s. They won all of the first five European Cups. In the 1960 final they defeated Eintracht Frankfurt by a record scoreline of 7-3.

Q Which country has the best national side?

A Between 1958 and 1970 Brazil won the World Cup three times. They were also winners in 1994. The team that beat Italy 4-1 in the 1970 World Cup Final was probably the best of all time, and included players such as Pelé and Jairzinho.

Q Who are the best in Europe today?

A AC Milan have had the strongest team in Europe in recent years. They have won the European Cup three times since 1989 and the Italia Seria A title for the last two years.

Q Which is the best team in England now?

A Manchester United won the Premier Division title in 1993. In 1994 they also won the FA Cup as well as the Premier Division title. This is known as 'the double', and is very hard to do. Manchester United have many exciting players, such as the young star, Ryan Giggs.

Peter Shilton is considered by many to have been the world's best goalkeeper.

Who was the greatest?

There have been many great footballers but there are a few who stand out as being better or more skilful than the rest. Fans frequently argue about who is the greatest player.

Q How do we know who are the best players?

A In Europe the European Player of the Year award is given to the player whom experts agree has been the best that year. Frenchman Michel Platini is the only footballer to have won the award three years running (1983-85). He was team captain when France won the European Championships in 1984.

Q Has anyone come close to Pelé?

A Many people think that the Argentinian, Diego Maradona, was almost as good as Pelé. He appeared in four World Cups and led his country to victory in the 1986 World Cup Final. Maradona was sent home from the 1994 World Cup for drug abuse, but will always be remembered as a great player.

Q Who was Edson Arantes do Nascimento?

A Edson Arantes do Nascimento is more commonly known by his nickname, Pelé. Pelé helped Brazil to win two World Cups (1958 and 1970) and scored 1,283 goals during his professional career. He was the most exciting attacking player ever and probably the best player in the world.

Sometimes players have objects named after them, or statues of them made. One of the most impressive statues is that of Newcastle United and England player, Jackie Milburn, which can be found in the middle of Newcastle upon Tyne city centre.

Kevin Keegan had a Royal Navy helicopter named after his nickname, 'Special K'.

Kevin Keegan

Q **Which British players have won European Player of the Year?**

A Only four British players have won the award. Three of them - Denis Law, Bobby Charlton and George Best - played for the Manchester United side of the 1960s. Kevin Keegan is the only one to have won the award twice.

Q **Who were the greatest European players?**

A There are two outstanding European players. Johan Cruyff of Holland won European Footballer of the Year three times, and was an excellent midfield player. Germany's Franz Beckenbauer is the only man to win the World Cup as a player (1974) and as a manager (1990).

Johan Cruyff

Q **Who is the best British player?**

A Ryan Giggs who plays for Manchester United is the most exciting player of his generation. Only in his early twenties, he is a lightning fast winger with skills second to none in the Premier league!

United's Ryan Giggs played for Wales when he was only 17 years old.

Q **Who is the best player in the world today?**

A Roberto Baggio, an Italian striker who plays for Juventus, is the world's top player. He scored important goals that helped Italy to a place in the 1994 World Cup Final, but will be remembered for missing the penalty that lost them the trophy.

What do players play for?

The original FA Cup was nicknamed the Little Tin Idol. It was stolen in 1895 never to be seen again.

Teams play in cup competitions to win trophies and in leagues to win the championship title.

Q What is the difference between a cup and a league?

A A cup is a knockout competition where only the winner goes through to the next round of matches. When there are only two teams left, they play against each other in the cup final. In a league, all the teams play one another and are awarded points for victories. The team with the most points wins the championship title.

Q Which team has won the FA Cup the most times?

A Tottenham Hotspur and Manchester United have both won the Cup eight times.

Gary Mabbutt, the Tottenham captain holds aloft the FA Cup in 1991.

Q Which is the best football league?

A The Italian first division, or 'Seria A' as it is known, is generally considered to contain the best and most skilful teams. The German 'Bundesliga' is also a very competitive league.

Bayern Munich are one of the strongest teams in the Bundesliga.

Q Which is the oldest football league?

A The English League Championship was first played for in 1888. The first champions were Preston North End.

The Copa Libertadores is the most important club competition in South America. Ten different countries in South America take part, sending the top two clubs from each country to compete for the cup.

The Royal Engineers team were one of the most successful early clubs and were famous for their teamwork.

Q **What is the oldest cup competition?**

A The English Football Association Cup (the FA Cup) is the world's oldest cup competition. It first took place in 1871 between the Royal Engineers and the Wanderers.

Q **Are there international cup competitions?**

A The European football organisation, UEFA, organises cup competitions between the best teams in all the countries in Europe. There are three European competitions: the European Cup, the Cup Winners' Cup, and the UEFA Cup.

Q **Which is the best cup that a club can win?**

A The European Cup is the most prestigious cup that a club can win as it features all of the league champions in Europe.

Cup Winners' Cup

UEFA Cup

European Cup

What is the World Cup?

The World Cup is the most important competition in football. It is an international event and the finals are held every four years. The winners really are the best footballing country in the world.

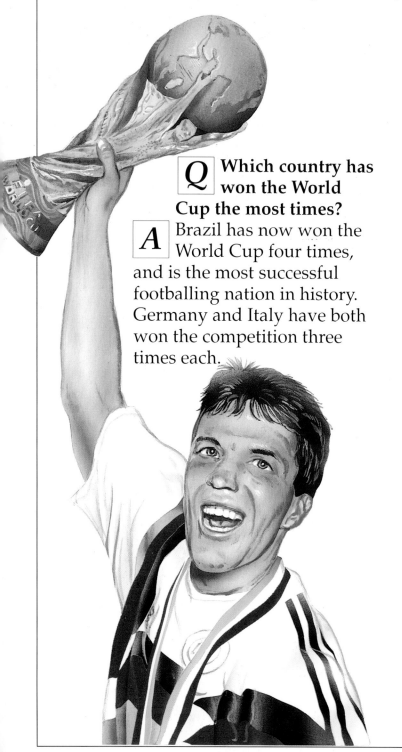

Q Which country has won the World Cup the most times?

A Brazil has now won the World Cup four times, and is the most successful footballing nation in history. Germany and Italy have both won the competition three times each.

Uruguay and Argentina in the 1930 final.

Q When was the first World Cup?

A The tournament first took place in 1930 and was held in Uruguay, South America. The winners of the tournament were Uruguay.

Q How is the World Cup organised?

A FIFA, the Fédération Internationale de Football Association, decides on the rules and organises the tournament. Only 24 teams can go to the finals, so qualifying groups are organised to select who goes. Teams that do well in their qualifying group go to the finals.

Up to 1994, only six teams had won the World Cup. They were: Brazil (four times), Italy (three times), Germany (three times), Argentina (twice), Uruguay (twice), and England (once).

Q Who has appeared in the most World Cups?

A Brazil. They are the only country to have qualified for every World Cup finals tournament since the competition began.

Q Has anybody ever scored a hat trick (three goals) in the final?

A Geoff Hurst, the England player, is the only person to have scored a hat trick in the World Cup final. His goals helped England to beat Germany 4-2 in extra time during the 1966 final.

Geoff Hurst scoring his hat trick in the 1966 final.

Q Which was the best World Cup?

A When the finals were held in Mexico in 1970, England, West Germany, Brazil and Italy all looked as though they could win the competition. It was the most exciting World Cup tournament seen so far. Brazil eventually became World Champions when they beat Italy 4-1 in the final.

Q When was FIFA founded?

A FIFA was founded in 1904. Originally there were only seven members. They were Belgium, Denmark, France, Holland, Spain, Sweden and Switzerland. England did not join until two years later.

What happens at a football match?

Around 31 billion people watch the World Cup on television.

Match day at a football ground is a very hectic and exciting time. Apart from the thousands of people coming to watch the game, there are also people from newspapers, radio and television trying to set up their equipment before the game starts.

Q Who is in charge of crowd safety?

A Although the football club is responsible for crowd safety, the police recommend the number of officers who need to be present at a match. The club then has to pay for the use of these officers. The club also provides stewards who help to control the crowds.

Q Where do the teams get changed?

A The teams get changed in dressing rooms inside the football ground. The home team and the visiting team have separate dressing rooms. The visiting team's dressing room is usually smaller than the home team's, and not as comfortable.

Q What is a ballboy?

A Ballboys and girls are usually members of the youth team or junior supporters' club. Their job is to retrieve the ball when it goes out of play during the match.

Q What do players eat before a match?

A Each player has their own favourite food which they eat before a match, be it bananas, mashed potato, or even cornflakes! Italian clubs keep a strict watch on what their players eat. Their diet consists of food high in carbohydrates, such as pasta, which provides energy. Players tend to eat at least an hour before the game begins to allow their food to digest.

The first match to be televised live was in 1936 in Germany. A year later the first live match in Britain to be televised took place between Arsenal and Everton.

Modern day cameras are very light and manoeuvrable. Some cameras even run along rails at the side of the pitch.

Q Where are the television cameras positioned?

A Television companies use large fixed cameras to broadcast football matches. The cameras are usually fixed to a special platform on top of one of the stands. Small cameras are also fixed inside the back of the goal to show goals and exciting goal mouth action.

Q Who else works on match day?

A There are more people working on match day than you might think. They include ticket and programme sellers, catering staff, First Aiders to take care of injuries, journalists, and even a disc jockey to play records during intervals in the game and make announcements. Also, before and after the match the groundstaff have to make sure that the pitch is in good condition and the stadium is tidy.

Q What does the manager do during a match?

A Before the match the manager explains to the team the tactics he wants them to use for the coming game. During the game he watches the game from the dugout (where the substitutes sit at the side of the field), or from the main stand. At half time he gives the players another team talk. The manager also sends on substitutes during a game when players get injured or tired.

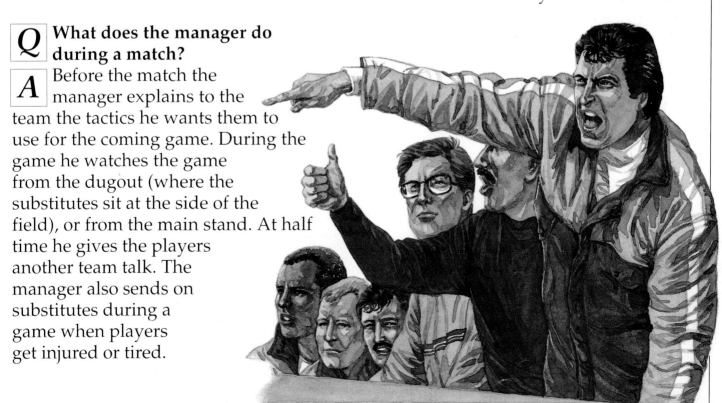

Do women play football?

The first official international match took place between England and Scotland in 1972.

Women have been playing football throughout history, and now play in organised leagues all around the world.

Q Was women's football popular?

A Women's football was very popular during the 1890s. Matches were better attended than some of the men's games, when people watched in tens of thousands. Attendances gradually declined, but are again on the increase.

Q When did women first play football?

A The earliest recorded instances of women playing football date from the 1500s. However, it seems likely that they were playing long before then.

Q What did they wear?

A Even though women were taking part in sport, they still had to wear long skirts, as it was considered immodest to show their legs. A picture of the British Ladies team of 1895 shows them wearing big heavy skirts, hitched up to allow them to kick the ball. They also wore shin guards, heavy shirts and nightcaps.

Doncaster Belles and Millwall Lionesses are two of the great modern sides in the English game. Both sides are more successful than their male counterparts and have won the Women's FA Cup numerous times.

Q **What did the football authorities think of women's football?**

A To begin with, the Football Association and the Football League were not keen on women playing football. In 1902, the FA decided that women's teams could not join the Association, and also banned mixed matches. In 1921, the Football League banned women's teams from using League grounds to play on. Later, both the FA and the League adopted a more positive attitude to women's football. FIFA and UEFA both officially recognised women's football in 1971.

Q **Do women play in every country?**

A Most countries have a women's league of some description. The game is very popular in Italy where there are professional teams.

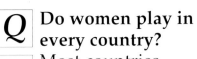

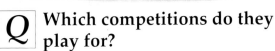

Q **Which competitions do they play for?**

A There are league competitions in most countries. There are also international matches, in particular the World Cup which was first held in China in 1991, which the USA won.

Q **Who was Rose Reilly?**

A Rose Reilly was the star player for a Scottish boy's team - without anyone realising she was a girl! She was one of the most skilful members of the team and would have played professionally had she been a boy. Other famous players include England captain, Gillian Coultard, the country's most capped player.

The first floodlights were used at Bramall Lane, Sheffield, in 1878.

What are stadiums used for?

A stadium is the building where a football team play. Usually, it is also the headquarters of the football club itself. Modern stadiums also have restaurants and offices attached to them as well, to try to get as much use out of the buildings as possible.

Q Why is the Giuseppe Meazza stadium so impressive?

A The Giuseppe Meazza Stadium, or the San Siro as it used to be known, is one of the most spectacular grounds in the world. Many architects have used the distinctive home of both Milan teams as the basis for modern day stadiums. The stadium was ahead of its time in design terms - the building we see today was actually built in the 1950s.

Q What was the Hillsborough disaster?

A During a FA Cup semi-final in 1989 at Sheffield Wednesday's ground, Hillsborough, 95 people were crushed to death and 170 injured when the terraces (standing area) at one end of the ground became overcrowded. As a result football grounds had to replace all standing areas with seats.

Giuseppe Meazza Stadium

There is a train buried beneath the pitch at Wembley! It was left behind when the ground was being built.

Q What are the 'Twin Towers'?

A The 'Twin Towers' is a nickname for Wembley Stadium in London. It refers to the two towers which stand on either side of the main entrance. Wembley is the biggest stadium in Britain with a capacity of 80,000.

Q Which is the biggest stadium in the world?

A The Maracaña Municipal Stadium in Rio de Janeiro, Brazil, is the biggest stadium in the world. It can hold up to 205,000 people.

Q What is a 'plastic pitch'?

A 'Plastic pitch' is the term used to describe an artificial surface used instead of grass. Some British teams laid artificial pitches during the 1980s. However, they did not prove popular and were later banned in the Premier League. The last plastic pitch in England was dug up in 1994.

Q What is a 'fanzine'?

A A 'fanzine' is a magazine produced by fans of a particular sport or pastime. Football fanzines became very popular in the 1980s as fans were frustrated at their lack of involvement in the major decisions being made on the game in general. Most fanzines are very critical of footballing authorities, and often make fun of players.

Q Do youth teams play in stadiums?

A If a youth team is connected to a major club they are usually allowed to use the ground when the professional sides are not using it. Youth football is played by under-18s, and is structured along similar lines to the professional game. There is even a Youth World Cup which started in 1977.

What is a statistic?

The fastest international goal was scored after ten seconds when San Marino scored against England in 1994.

A statistic is a piece of information, such as a goal-scoring record, for example. Statistics allow people to compare the performances of players or teams throughout history.

Q Who scored the fastest goal?

A Jim Fryatt of Bradford City is supposed to have scored a goal after only four seconds from the start!

Q What is the highest score in a game?

A Arbroath beat Bon Accord 36-0 in a Scottish Cup match in 1885. Seven further goals were disallowed for off-side! It is likely that more goals would have been scored, but as goal nets were not used at that point a lot of time was wasted retrieving the ball after a goal was scored.

Q What is the record for most goals in a season?

A William Ralph 'Dixie' Dean of Everton scored an incredible 60 goals in 39 games during the 1927-28 season. He broke the old record of 59 goals in the last game of the season.

Q Who scored the fastest ever own goal?

A Pat Kruse of Torquay United headed the ball into his own net after only six seconds of their game against Cambridge United.

The highest score ever recorded at a football match was not allowed to stand. The match took place in the former Yugoslavia, between Ilinden and Mladost, which Ilinden won 134-1! However it turned out that Ilinden had bribed both the referee and the Mladost team!

Tommy Walker and Freddie Steele, scorers for Scotland and England.

Q What was the highest crowd for a game in Britain?

A Officially, the highest crowd attendance in Britain was the 149,547 people who watched the Scotland v England match at Hampden Park in 1937. However, it is estimated that 160,000 people watched the 1923 FA Cup final between Bolton Wanderers and West Ham.

Q What was the highest crowd attendance in the world?

A An amazing 199,589 people watched the Brazil v Uruguay World Cup match at the Maracaña Municipal Stadium in 1950.

Q Who is the world's most expensive player?

A Gianluigi Lentini of Italy is the world's most expensive player. A C Milan paid Torino £13 million for Lentini in 1992.

William 'Fatty' Foulkes weighed an amazing 146 kg! Foulkes played in goal for Sheffield United and England.

Who was Pickles?

Pickles was the dog who rescued the World Cup trophy! In 1966 the trophy was stolen from an exhibition in London, and Pickles found it under a bush while out for a walk with his owner.

Q Where is the World Cup trophy now?

A No one knows! The original trophy was given to Brazil to keep in 1970, but was stolen in 1983 and never found. It is thought that the solid gold trophy may have been melted down.

Q What is the record score in a World Cup game?

A New Zealand beat Fiji by an amazing 13-0 in a World Cup qualifying game in 1981.

Q Has a referee ever scored a goal?

A In 1968, referee Ivan Robinson accidentally scored the winning goal for Barrow in a Third Division game against Plymouth Argyle.

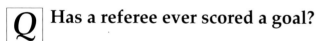

The autobiography of Len Shackleton, the Newcastle United and Sunderland player, had a chapter called 'What the average director knows about football'. The chapter was blank!

All clubs have nicknames that are usually based on either their history or the colour of strip. For example, AC Milan are the Red Devils, Newcastle United are the Magpies, and the Australian team are the Socceroos.

Q Which player has been sent off the most times?

A Scottish footballer Willie Johnston was shown the red card 15 times during his professional career.

Q Do referees ever get injured?

A Sometimes they do get quite seriously hurt. Trevor Brooking, the West Ham player, once accidentally knocked out the referee during a match!

Q Has a goalkeeper ever scored a goal?

A There have been a few goalkeepers who have scored own goals, but some 'keepers have managed to score for their own side. In 1923-24, Chesterfield goalie, Arnold Birch, scored five penalty goals in one season. In the 1967 Charity Shield game, Tottenham goalkeeper, Pat Jennings, scored a goal from his own penalty area.

Q Have any famous people ever played football?

A One of the most famous is Pope John Paul II, who used to play in goal for a Polish football team.

Index